Published 1982 by Warwick Press,
730 Fifth Avenue, New York, New York 10019.

First published in Great Britain by
Kingfisher Books Limited, 1981.

Copyright © 1981 by Grisewood & Dempsey Ltd.

Printed in Portugal by Gris Impressores
S.A.R.L., Cacém.

Library of Congress Catalog Card No. 81–51791

ISBN 0–531–09195–3

THE TIME OF THE PROPHETS

David Kent

Adviser:
Reverend Graham Mitchell

Illustrated by
**Harry Bishop, John Keay
and Rob McCaig**

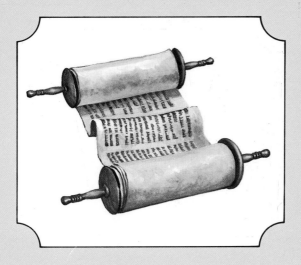

WARWICK PRESS

Book 4: The Time of the Prophets

THE PROPHETS described in the Bible were mainly stern, poor, God-fearing men. They disliked the rich, lazy life led by most of their country's kings—especially kings who forgot their own God and worshiped the Gods of other countries instead. One after another, prophets warned how God would punish such disobedience.

Sure enough, punishments followed. By the time of the prophets, Solomon's empire had split up. Foreign invaders destroyed Israel in the north, and later the southern kingdom of Judah was also defeated. For a time its Jewish people were captives in far-off Babylon. But prophets like Ezekiel kept alive the people's faith in God, and the hope of rebuilding their kingdom.

Naboth's Vineyard

Ahab of Israel was a weak, selfish king who felt he should have whatever he wanted. One day his fancy strayed to a vineyard next to the palace. The land belonged to one of his subjects, called Naboth.

Summoning Naboth, Ahab said airily, "Your vineyard would make me a handy vegetable garden. I'll buy it for more than it's worth."

But Naboth refused to sell. "That land has belonged to my family for generations," he said.

Ahab felt so angry at being turned down, he sulked like a child. But his wife Jezebel was tougher.

"Don't worry, I'll get you that vineyard," she promised. And the cruel queen secretly ordered dishonest judges to find Naboth guilty of treason and have him executed.

When this was done, Jezebel told Ahab, "You can have Naboth's vineyard now—the man's dead."

Ahab's greedy eyes lit up with joy; but not for long. As the king gloated over his new possession the stern prophet Elijah appeared.

Ahab was afraid of Elijah; when he showed up it was always to punish the king for disobeying God. This time proved worst of all.

"I bring God's curse for the wrong you have done!" thundered Elijah. "Your family will die and be food for wild beasts."

Ahab begged God's forgiveness, but it was too late, he and his family all came to violent ends.

3

The Parting of Elijah and Elisha

Elijah the prophet grew old and knew he must soon die. But he did not want to worry his friend Elisha. So Elijah just said, "Wait here while I go on a journey."

But Elisha replied, "I'll go wherever you go." For Elisha had guessed what was going to happen.

Each time they came to a town, Elijah asked Elisha to wait, and each time he refused. At last they stood by the River Jordan, watched by 50 young men who admired Elijah's work as God's messenger.

"Stay here while I go across on God's business," Elijah ordered. But Elisha would not be left behind.

As the young men watched with amazement, Elijah struck the river with his rolled cloak and the water parted. Then the two prophets walked across on dry land.

At the far side, Elijah knew his end was near. He sadly asked, "What is your last wish before I am taken away from you?"

Elisha answered, "To be twice as powerful a prophet as you."

"Your wish will be granted if you see me go," came the answer. Suddenly a dazzling glow shone between them and became fiery horses pulling a fiery chariot.

Elisha gasped with astonishment, for Elijah seemed to be swept up with the chariot as it soared into the sky and then vanished.

Only Elijah's cloak was left to show where the prophet had stood. Elisha nervously picked it up and turned back to the river. He struck it with the cloak as Elijah had done. Again the water parted. The watchers knew that although Elijah was dead, God's power lived on in Elisha.

The Death of Jezebel

The first tale in this book told of a murder planned by King Ahab's wife Jezebel. God punished this crime by killing the king and his sons one by one. But Jezebel herself was saved for a specially horrible kind of death.

God must have felt she deserved it. For Jezebel was a foreign princess who went on worshiping a foreign god after she married King Ahab and settled in Israel. Worse still, this determined woman tried to force the people of Israel to give up their God for hers.

The prophet Elisha chose a man called Jehu to punish Ahab's wife and surviving sons. Jehu was an officer in the Israelite army.

Elisha's message to Jehu was short, "You are to be king of Israel. But first you must kill off Ahab's family—especially Jezebel."

A man of action, Jehu wasted no time. He killed his own king (Ahab's son Joram) then galloped to the palace. Jezebel coldly watched him coming. Proud and defiant to the last, she made up her eyes and did her hair. Then she sat in an upstairs window and glared down at Jehu disdainfully.

"Do you come to make peace, then?" she sneered. Then she yelled "Murderer of your own master!"

Looking up, Jehu saw manservants behind her. "Throw her down!" he commanded. They did, for they knew that her cause was lost.

She fell among horses which reared and trampled her body. Later, jackals ate the remains. So there was simply no body left to bury.

Her punishment was terrible, but then so were her crimes.

Josiah and the Book of the Law

"Your Majesty, see what the high priest has just found in the temple!" His secretary carefully handed King Josiah of Judah some old yellow scrolls. (In those days people wrote on sheets made from the pith of papyrus reeds, and they rolled up each sheet for safekeeping.)

Josiah unrolled one scroll gingerly, for it was brittle with age. As he read, the king turned pale with terror. For the scroll set out some of God's laws that had long been forgotten—and worse than that, they had been most dreadfully disobeyed.

Kings like Josiah's own father and grandfather had been largely to blame. No one could say that grandfather Manasseh followed God's laws. He had practiced black magic. In God's own temple at Jerusalem he had built altars to heathen gods like the sun, moon and stars. He had even had his own son burnt to death as a gift for a heathen god.

At least Josiah himself had behaved better. He had repaired the temple, for instance. But even he had unknowingly broken some laws.

Josiah knew God punished disobedience severely. Maybe he was already preparing a storm, an earthquake or other frightful disasters.

The king nervously called his advisers together. He said, "Ask God what we should do. For we and our ancestors have not behaved as this book says we ought."

So the high priest, the king's secretary and other important officials set off to find Huldah, a prophetess well known as someone God used as a messenger.

They came back with very bad news of God's plans: "I shall destroy Jerusalem and make the land desolate. But because you are sorry for what has happened, Josiah, I shall wait until you are dead."

Josiah Reads the Laws

Josiah at once called a great meeting. Priests, prophets, rich men and poor —thousands swarmed into Jerusalem. Soon a vast crowd packed the space in front of the temple. A great murmuring arose as the mystified citizens asked one another what was going to happen.

Silence fell as the king appeared by the temple door. Josiah unrolled the first scroll. Then, one by one, he read out God's laws in a clear, loud voice for all to hear.

Afterwards the king made the people join him in promising to obey all God's commands from then on.

Josiah was as good as his word. He emptied the temple of all signs of heathen worship. He smashed heathen altars and idols all over the land. He even had heathen priests put to death. The people of Judah had never been so faithful to God, as when Josiah was king.

Jeremiah's Warnings

"If we stay shut up here we'll all be killed, or die of disease or hunger," warned Jeremiah. King Zedekiah of Judah could not disagree with God's prophet, for he knew that a huge Babylonian army surrounded Jerusalem. Before long the city would have to stop fighting.

Yet Zedekiah stubbornly refused to admit he was beaten. And he lost patience with anyone who preached defeat. Zedekiah was especially annoyed with Jeremiah; the prophet seldom opened his mouth without moaning of some disaster ahead.

So Zedekiah grew very angry indeed when Jeremiah went on to say, "If you surrender, God will make sure that our lives are spared."

What Jeremiah said was just commonsense, but to Zedekiah it sounded like treason.

Jerusalem's city officials shared this suspicion, so the king did not care when they had Jeremiah flogged and thrown in a dungeon.

Jeremiah lay there in the dark, half-starved, for several days. Then Zedekiah had him brought out.

"Any message from God?" he asked.

"Yes," replied Jeremiah. "The Babylonians will defeat you." Then Jeremiah asked, "Why have you put me in prison? I have never done anyone any harm. Don't send me back to that dungeon—I'll die."

So Zedekiah relented a little. Instead of the dungeon, Jeremiah found himself in the palace prison—a more comfortable jail. And while there was bread to spare he got a small loaf each day.

But things quickly got worse for Jeremiah when word went around that he still expected defeat. Men complained to the king. "His treacherous prophecies will make our troops lose heart," they said. "He must die!"

So Zedekiah let them drag Jeremiah from his cell and put him into a well. It was empty, but Jeremiah found himself sinking into a soft, smelly layer of mud in the bottom. There he was left without food.

The Rescue

Jeremiah would surely have died but for a kind African palace official named Ebed-melech. When he learnt what had happened, he pleaded with Zedekiah to have Jeremiah brought up. Once more the king changed his mind and relented.

Soon Jeremiah heard voices above. Then something came snaking down into the well. Men were lowering old, soft rags tied to ropes.

"Tie the rags under your armpits," shouted Ebed-melech. "They'll stop the ropes chafing your skin."

Jeremiah obeyed, and they hauled him up. Then it was back to jail. Jeremiah was still in prison when the Babylonians swarmed into the city, just as he had said they would.

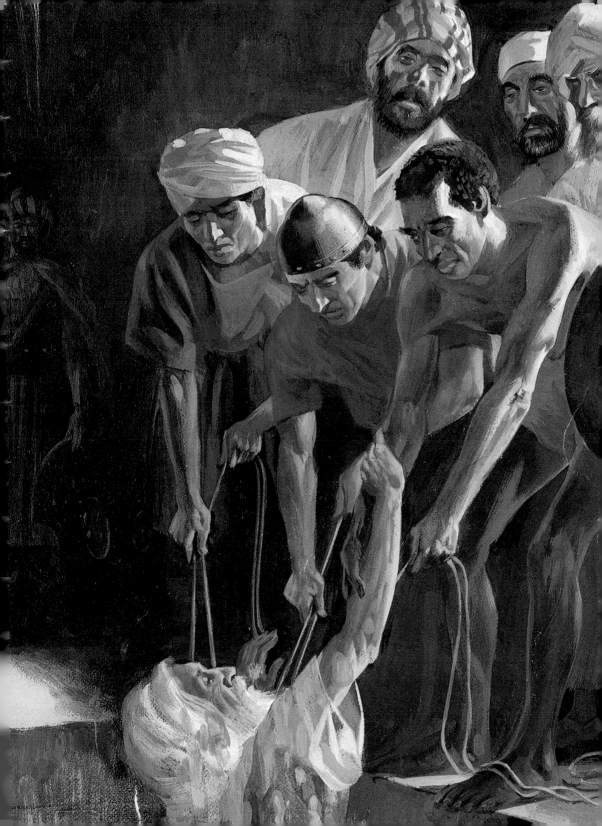

Zedekiah

King Zedekiah gazed hopelessly around him. Everywhere he saw the thin, drawn faces of people who had hardly eaten for weeks. Now the last food had gone; death from hunger seemed certain. Jerusalem still held out against the Babylonian army, but the end was close.

Zedekiah made a last desperate plan. He would take his troops and break out at night while the enemy slept. Maybe he hoped to fetch help, but he was fated to fail.

After dark, the king and his men bored a hole in the city wall, burst out of Jerusalem, and made for the Jordan valley. But they hadn't a chance. Babylonian troops were soon pounding hard in pursuit. Weak

with hunger, the king and his men were easily overtaken and seized.

Zedekiah found himself dragged in front of Nebuchadnezzar. The pitiless Babylonian king pronounced terrible punishments.

Zedekiah was forced to watch his sons being killed. Then he was blinded, put in chains and marched off to Babylon. It was inhuman, yet he could hardly complain; Jeremiah the prophet had warned what would happen if Zedekiah defied Babylon.

Not only the king suffered. His subjects were herded in thousands and hauled off to Babylon too. Meanwhile troops smashed the temple and Jerusalem's other fine buildings—even its walls.

King gone, capital smashed, land half emptied of people—the nation of Judah seemed finished.

The Valley of Bones

Among the thousands of captives who trudged the dusty roads from Judah to Babylon was a tough, clear-thinking man—the prophet Ezekiel. Ezekiel was determined that whatever happened, his people should never forget their God or homeland.

This wasn't easy. Life became pleasant in Babylon for many Jews, as the people of Judah were now called. It was true they had foreign masters, but Babylon was rich, and anyone clever or skilled had a chance to find a good job. Jews became successful businessmen, lawyers and manufacturers—some even became courtiers.

They also found much to admire, for Babylon was a splendid city to live in. Fine villas and palaces lined the banks of the great Euphrates river. There were broad avenues, tall city walls, and magnificent buildings with immense metal gates. Plants of all kinds grew in the great hanging gardens—one of the wonders of the world.

Soaring above all this was a high tower, a square-sided, man-made mountain of brick, rising by giant steps—each step painted a different color. On top stood a room said to be visited by a god.

Ezekiel warned the Jews against worshiping all such foreign gods. But he did much more than that. He offered Jews hope for the future. Perhaps best of all, he promised that one day God would give them back their lost homeland under the rule of a just king.

This was not wishful thinking. In a strange waking dream Ezekiel had seen what was going to happen. This is how he explained it.

"I seemed to be in a valley full of the scattered bones of human skeletons. The Spirit of God took me among them, and asked me, 'Can these dead bones ever come alive again?'

"I replied, 'Only you can answer that question, Lord.'

"Then the Spirit told me to say to the bones, 'Dry bones, God says he will clothe you with muscles and skin, and breathe life back into your bodies.' So I said all that."

The Bones Live Again

"When I stopped speaking I heard a strange rattling. Suddenly the scattered bones were coming together to make whole skeletons. And this was just the start. Sinews and flesh and skin all joined the bones and made people—but only dead ones.

"Then God's Spirit said, 'Call up the winds and breathe life into these dead bodies.'

"So I did, and the bodies began breathing. Then they stood up, and suddenly the valley was filled by a vast living crowd."

In this way Ezekiel told the Jews that their own dead kingdom would live again. And he was right.

Daniel in the Lion's Den

The jailers seized Daniel and threw him into a den of hungry lions. In moments their teeth must surely be crunching his bones. Yet only hours before Daniel had been one of the most powerful men in the entire Persian Empire.

What had happened was this. Daniel had been living in Babylon when the Persians invaded and made it part of the largest empire the world had yet seen. It was too big for the emperor, Darius, to run alone. So he ruled through 120 governors—one for each of his empire's provinces. In charge of these governors he placed three presidents. The wisest was Daniel—so wise that Darius planned to put Daniel in charge of the rest. This made the others jealous, for Daniel was a Jew—an outsider in the Persian Empire.

Daniel's enemies plotted to get rid of him. It proved difficult; he was so honest and loyal they could find no reason for persuading Darius to sack him. Then they remembered that Daniel was very religious, and said his prayers to the Jewish God—a different God from theirs.

One day some of Daniel's enemies visited the emperor and suggested a new law to test his subjects' loyalty. "Your majesty," they fawned, "we propose that any person asking a favor of anyone but yourself in the next 30 days shall be thrown to the lions in your zoo."

The unsuspecting Darius agreed. He soon regretted it, for they quickly came back to say Daniel was ignoring the new law by praying to God and asking him favors.

Darius was furious at having been tricked into killing his favorite subject. But there was no way he could undo the new law. So he sadly ordered Daniel's arrest, and walked with him to the mouth of the lion's den to say goodbye.

The emperor's voice broke with grief when he said to Daniel, "May your God save you." Darius felt sure he was seeing Daniel for the last time as the jailers pushed him inside the den.

Next Morning

Darius felt so wretched with worry that night, he could hardly sleep. Early next morning he ran to the lions' den. He knew it was hopeless, Daniel must be dead. Yet something made him call out, "Daniel, did your God save you?"

Darius gave a start of surprise as a voice from inside the den called back, "God kept me safe—the lions didn't touch me."

The emperor was overjoyed. He had Daniel brought out at once, and found him not even scratched. Then Darius threw Daniel's accusers to the lions. This time, no one came out alive.

Rebuilding Jerusalem

"What's the matter Nehemiah?" asked the Persian emperor. His Jewish cupbearer—a trusted official —was looking depressed.

"Bad news from home, your majesty," he replied. "I've just heard that the city of Jerusalem is in ruins."

You may remember that Babylonian troops had smashed the city when they drove out its people. But the Jews' Persian rulers proved kinder. So when Nehemiah asked permission to go home and rebuild Jerusalem, the Persian emperor agreed. He even lent Nehemiah some men to help him.

Nehemiah made his main task rebuilding the great outer walls that defended the city. But there was more than building work to be done. Fighting also seemed likely, for local leaders were jealous of Nehemiah and tried to stop the rebuilding.

A born organizer, Nehemiah had an answer for that. While half his men worked he made the rest stand guard close by. All kept their weapons handy, and slept fully dressed in case of night attack.

By day, work went on incredibly fast. Toiling from sunrise to sunset in the searing heat of late summer, the men rebuilt Jerusalem's walls in just 52 days.

Then, with Nehemiah as their new governor, the Jews of Jerusalem settled down to a new age of peace.

Jonah and the Great Fish

No prophet had a more terrifying adventure than Jonah—a man swallowed alive by a huge fish.

It was his own fault, of course; he had disobeyed God's orders.

God had told Jonah, "Go to the city of Nineveh in Assyria, and tell its people I shall destroy them."

But Jonah did not fancy the idea of trudging all the way to Assyria only to make its people hate him. So he ran away in the opposite direction. He bought a ticket for a boat sailing to Spain, then he climbed into the hold and fell fast asleep.

God, however, was not to be cheated. Soon the sky darkened, a fierce gale whipped up the waves, and the ship reared and plunged like a wild beast. Passengers and seamen screamed with fear. Sailors threw cargo overboard to lighten the vessel, and the captain made everyone pray to their gods, to please whichever angry god had sent the hurricane. But the storm raged on.

Then the captain found Jonah, still fast asleep. "Wake up!" bellowed the captain. "Up on deck and pray to your God to save us."

As soon as Jonah saw how bad the storm was, he knew what was really wrong with the ship.

"It's all my fault for disobeying my God—the only real God," Jonah confessed. "The one way to stop the storm is to throw me overboard."

Desperate with fear, the sailors agreed, and hurled Jonah into the raging sea. At once it calmed down.

As the waves closed over his head Jonah knew he was finished. Just time for a last prayer, then . . .

Suddenly came a loud gulping sound and Jonah felt himself sucked into a great, dark cave—a cave that rumbled and moved. He was inside the jaws of a whale-like fish.

For three days and nights poor Jonah crouched or squelched around in the smelly darkness. Then he prayed. His voice echoed spookily as

Jonah called out, "If you save me God, I'll do anything you want from now on."

Jonah's prayer was answered. He soon heard sand grating under the fish's belly. Then light dazzled his eyes as the monster's jaws gaped wide. The beast gave a giant cough, and Jonah found himself shot from the fish's mouth and towards a beach, like a cork from a popgun.

You can be sure that Jonah never again tried escaping from God.

The Sorrows of Job

The story of Job is one of great suffering. Job had to trust God no matter what happened—and the things that happened to Job were really terrible.

Job had always been a good, God-fearing man, and God rewarded him by making him rich. He owned thousands of camels and sheep, and hundreds of donkeys and cows. Scores of servants scurried about in his service. Job spent his wealth generously—he was always throwing big family parties.

God felt so proud of Job's goodness that he even told Satan about it. The evil angel was unimpressed.

"Job only worships you because you made him rich," he sneered. "Just let me make him poor, and *then* see what he calls you."

God agreed, so sure did he feel that Job would stay faithful. So Satan flew off and quickly got busy making Job's life a misery.

The first sign of things going badly wrong was an exhausted messenger who ran up to Job's house. "The Sabaeans have stolen your cattle and donkeys" he gasped. "They've killed all the herdsmen as well. I'm the only one who escaped."

Before he had finished, another man burst in, shouting "Lightning has struck your sheep and shepherds, and slaughtered the lot."

A third messenger arrived to say all Job's camels had been stolen. Then came the fourth and heaviest blow of all, the roof of a house had collapsed, killing all of Job's sons and daughters.

One moment Job had been a rich, happy, family man. Now he was suddenly poor, childless and half crazed with grief. Yet instead of blaming God, he said "God gave me all I had, so it was his to take away."

Satan could hardly believe his ears. But he refused to give up. He struck Job again. This time horribly painful boils broke out all over Job's body.

Job's wife felt bitterly angry. "Why don't you curse God?" she moaned. "It's all his fault."

Job felt so ill he wished he had never been born. Yet he only said, "We can't expect God to hand out pleasant things all the time."

Job's Comforters

Three friends who came to offer their sympathy proved even less help than Job's wife. They said things like, "Stop moaning! *You* must be to blame if God is punishing you. Good people don't suffer like this."

Job knew this was untrue. But each time he tried saying so his friends refused to believe him.

At last God brought the miseries to an end. He explained to Job that no man can always understand why suffering happens. Then God again gave Job, health, wealth and children. His patience had been rewarded.

Index

**Jeffersonville Township Public
Library**
P.O. Box 1548
Jeffersonville, IN 47131

DEMCO